T0417715

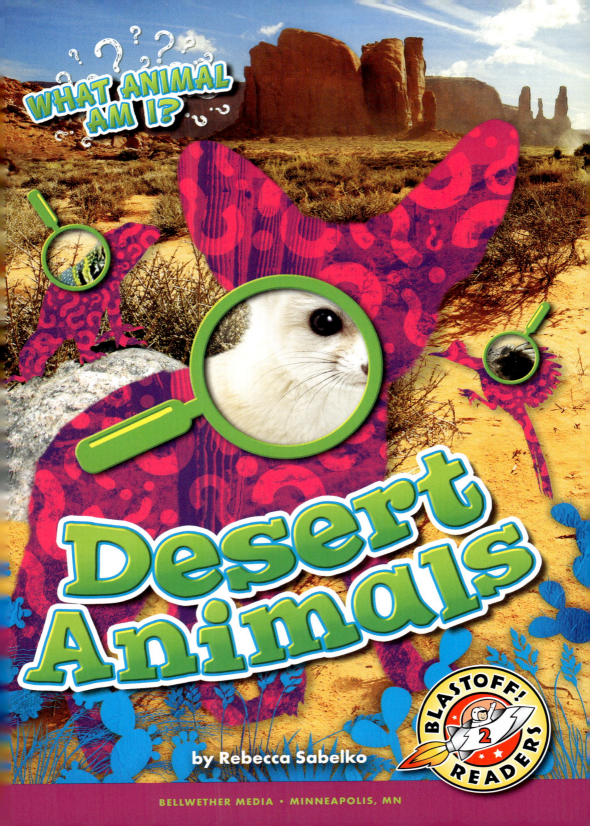

Desert Animals

by Rebecca Sabelko

BELLWETHER MEDIA • MINNEAPOLIS, MN

BLASTOFF! READERS

2

Blastoff! Readers are carefully developed by literacy experts to build reading stamina and move students toward fluency by combining standards-based content with developmentally appropriate text.

Level 1 provides the most support through repetition of high-frequency words, light text, predictable sentence patterns, and strong visual support.

Level 2 offers early readers a bit more challenge through varied sentences, increased text load, and text-supportive special features.

Level 3 advances early-fluent readers toward fluency through increased text load, less reliance on photos, advancing concepts, longer sentences, and more complex special features.

★ **Blastoff! Universe**

Reading Level

Grade
K

Grades
1–3

Grade
4

This edition first published in 2023 by Bellwether Media, Inc.

No part of this publication may be reproduced in whole or in part without written permission of the publisher. For information regarding permission, write to Bellwether Media, Inc., Attention: Permissions Department, 6012 Blue Circle Drive, Minnetonka, MN 55343.

Library of Congress Cataloging-in-Publication Data

Names: Sabelko, Rebecca, author.
Title: Desert Animals / by Rebecca Sabelko.
Description: Minneapolis, MN : Bellwether Media, Inc., 2023. | Series: What animal am I? |
   Includes bibliographical references and index. | Audience: Ages 5-8 | Audience: Grades 2-3 |
   Summary: "Relevant images match informative text in this introduction to different desert animals.
   Intended for students in kindergarten through third grade"-- Provided by publisher.
Identifiers: LCCN 2022009374 (print) | LCCN 2022009375 (ebook) | ISBN 9781644877265
   (library binding) | ISBN 9781648347726 (ebook)
Subjects: LCSH: Desert animals--Juvenile literature.
Classification: LCC QL116 .S233 2023 (print) | LCC QL116 (ebook) | DDC 591.754--dc23/eng/20220303
LC record available at https://lccn.loc.gov/2022009374
LC ebook record available at https://lccn.loc.gov/2022009375

Editor: Rachael Barnes   Designer: Brittany McIntosh

Printed in the United States of America, North Mankato, MN.

Table of Contents

Deserts are areas of dry land that receive little rain. They are often hot.

Many animals have **adapted** to the heat!

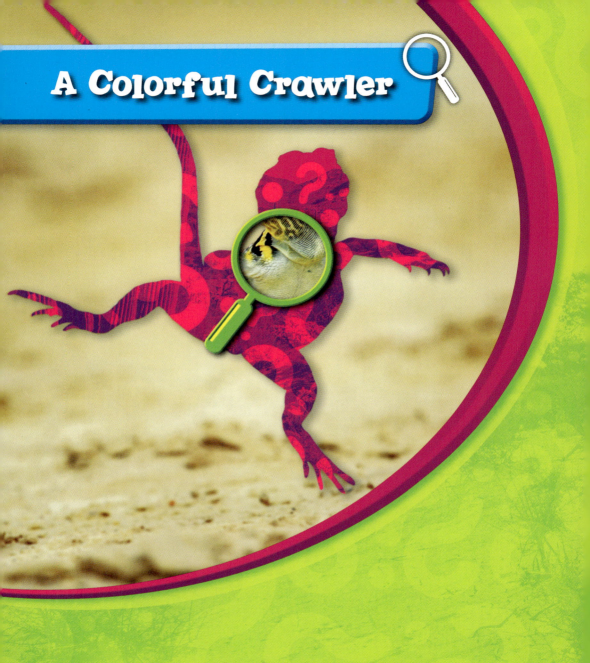

I am a colorful **reptile** that crawls across the deserts of North America.

I run on my strong back legs to escape **predators**.
What animal am I?

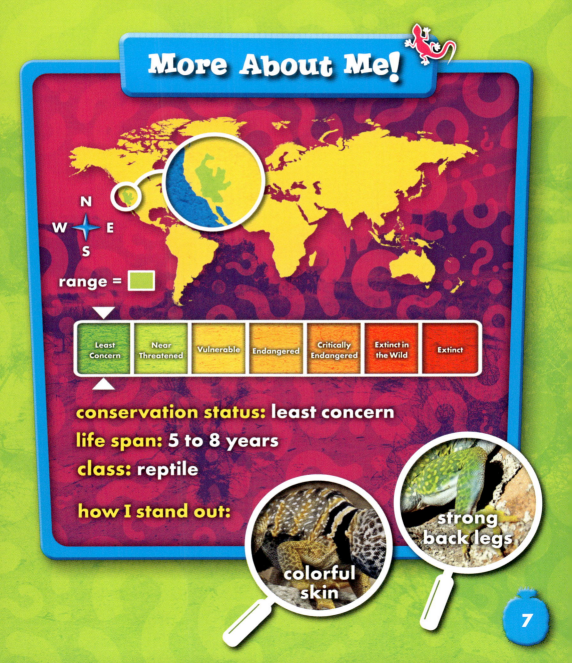

More About Me!

range =

Least Concern	Near Threatened	Vulnerable	Endangered	Critically Endangered	Extinct in the Wild	Extinct

conservation status: least concern

life span: 5 to 8 years

class: reptile

how I stand out:

colorful skin

strong back legs

I am a collared lizard!
I need sunshine to live.

I eat **insects** and
other small animals.
Heat helps me
digest food.

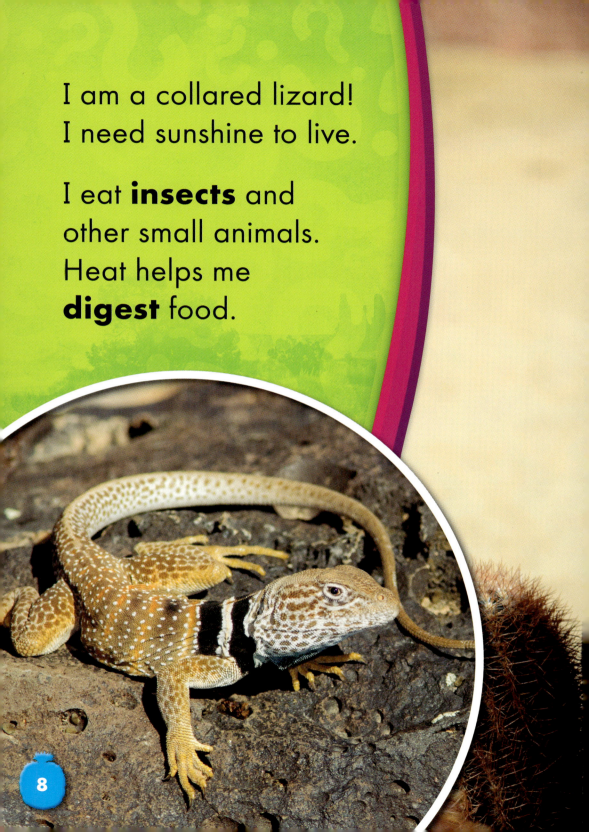

Collared Lizard Food

insects   spiders   lizards

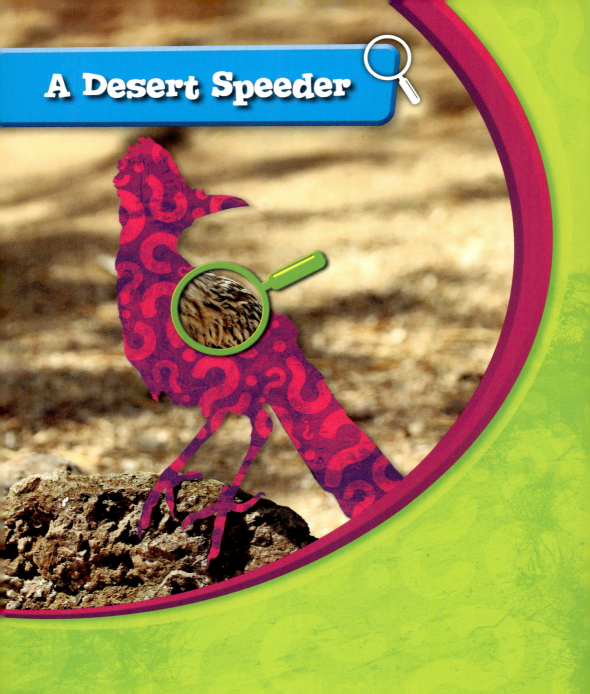

I am a large bird that lives on the ground.

My X-shaped feet are strong.
My legs are long. These parts
help me run! What animal am I?

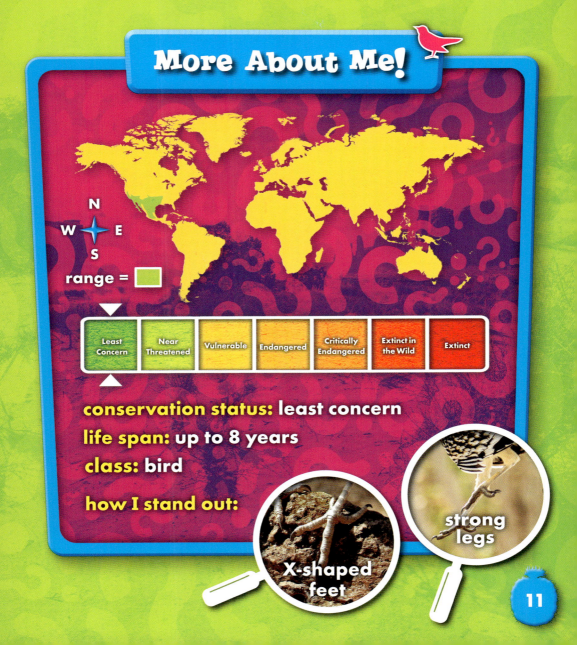

More About Me!

range =

Least Concern | Near Threatened | Vulnerable | Endangered | Critically Endangered | Extinct in the Wild | Extinct

conservation status: least concern

life span: up to 8 years

class: bird

how I stand out:

X-shaped feet

strong legs

Greater Roadrunner Food

snakes   lizards   insects

12

I am a greater roadrunner!
I zoom past cactuses
and rocks in the desert.

I chase tasty snakes
and lizards at high speeds!

13

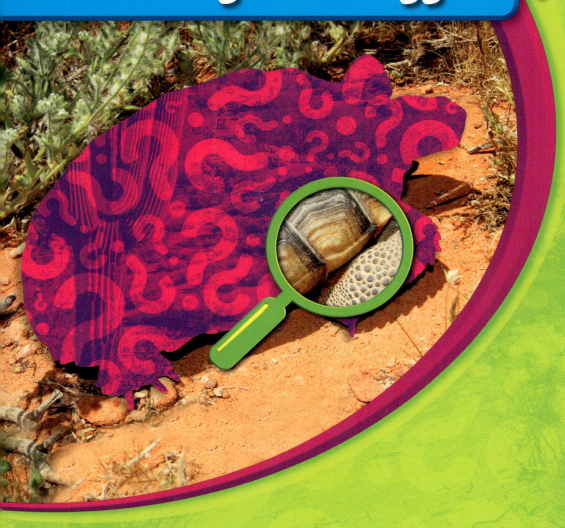

I am a reptile. I can pull my head and legs inside my hard shell.

I live much of my life underground.
What animal am I?

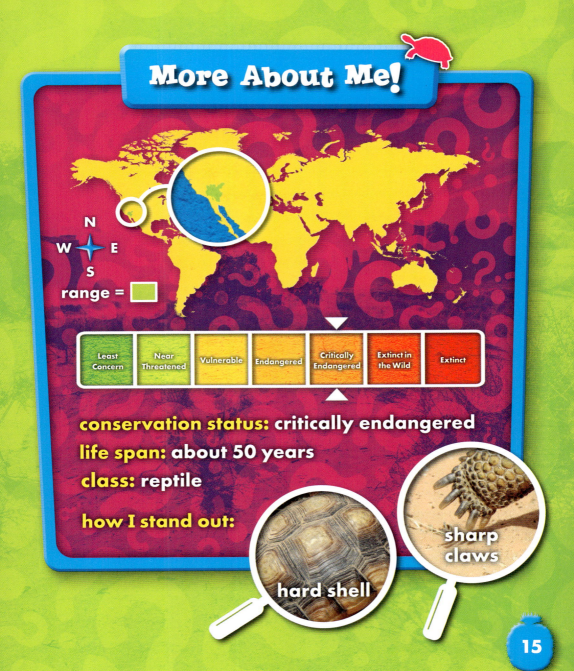

More About Me!

range =

Least Concern | Near Threatened | Vulnerable | Endangered | Critically Endangered | Extinct in the Wild | Extinct

conservation status: critically endangered

life span: about 50 years

class: reptile

how I stand out:

hard shell

sharp claws

I am a desert tortoise!
I come out of my
burrow to munch on
grass and cactuses.

I have sharp claws.
They help me dig
through sand!

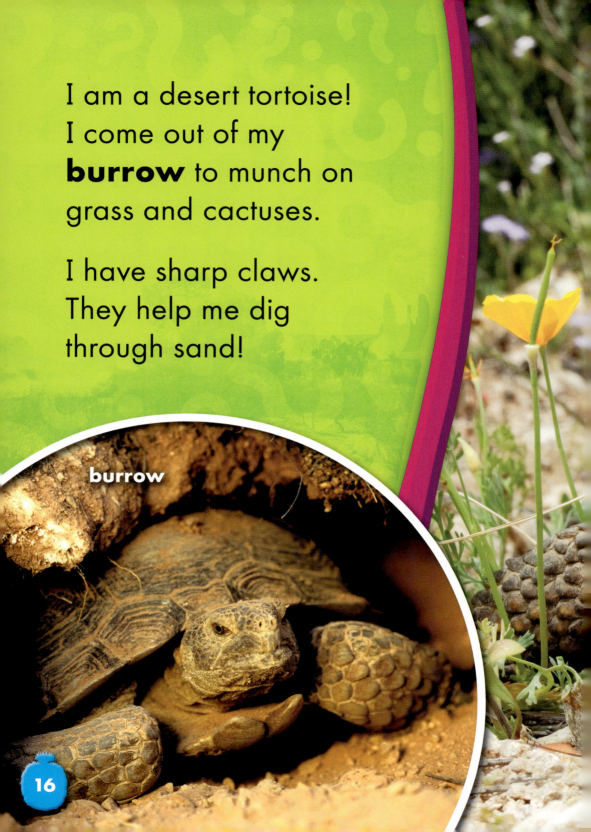

burrow

Desert Tortoise Food

grass   cactuses   wildflowers

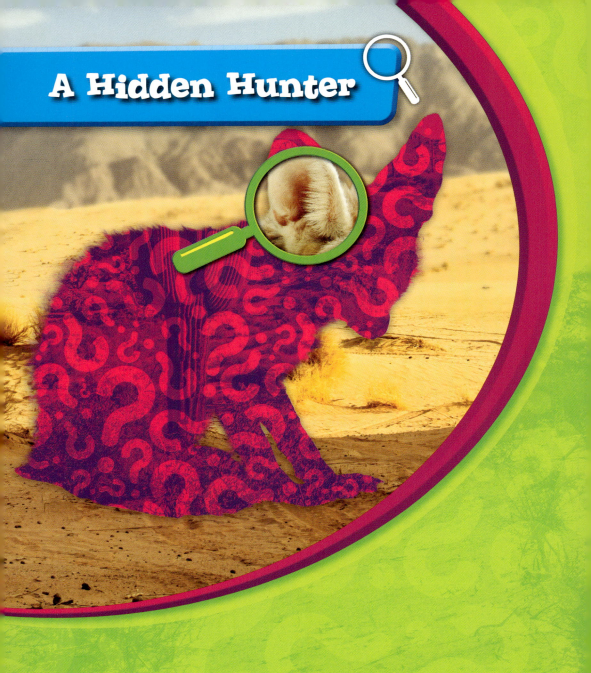

I am a **mammal** that lives in the Sahara Desert.

My fur is the color of sand.
It covers the bottoms of my feet!
What animal am I?

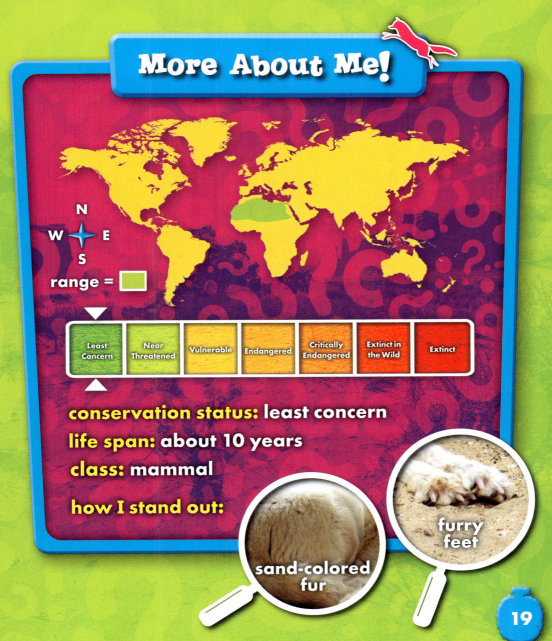

More About Me!

range =

| Least Concern | Near Threatened | Vulnerable | Endangered | Critically Endangered | Extinct in the Wild | Extinct |

conservation status: least concern

life span: about 10 years

class: mammal

how I stand out:

sand-colored fur

furry feet

Fennec Fox Food

rodents insects birds

I am a fennec fox! My huge ears keep me cool. They also help me hear **rodents** under the sand.

I live well in my desert home!

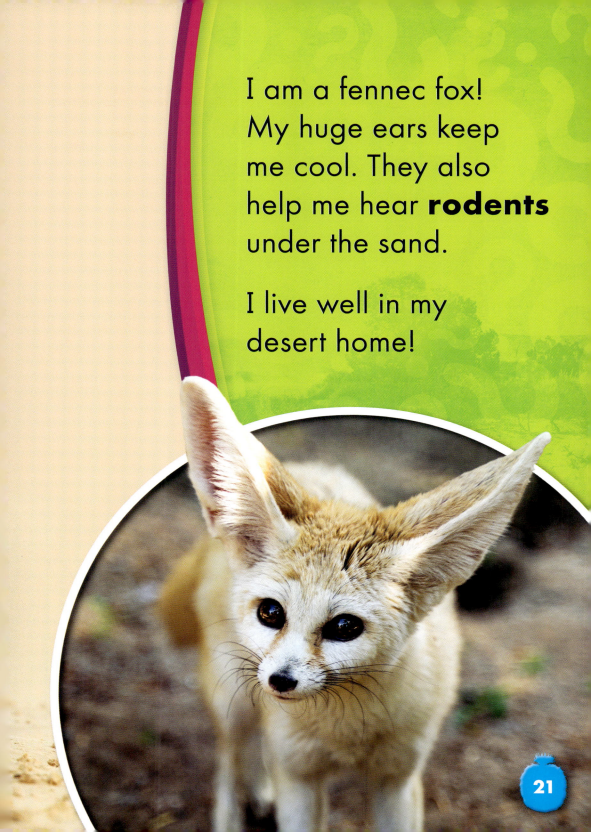

Glossary

adapted—changed over a long period of time

burrow—a tunnel or hole in the ground used as an animal's home

digest—to break down food

insects—small animals with six legs and hard outer bodies; an insect's body is divided into three parts.

mammal—a warm-blooded animal that has a backbone and feeds its young milk

predators—animals that hunt other animals for food

reptile—a cold-blooded animal that has a backbone and lays eggs

rodents—small animals that gnaw on their food; mice, rats, and squirrels are all rodents.

To Learn More

AT THE LIBRARY

Murray, Julie. *Animals in Deserts*. Minneapolis, Minn.: Abdo Kids, 2021.

Perish, Patrick. *Fennec Foxes*. Minneapolis, Minn.: Bellwether Media, 2019.

Rusick, Jessica. *Animals Hidden in the Desert*. North Mankato, Minn.: Pebble, 2022.

ON THE WEB

FACTSURFER

Factsurfer.com gives you a safe, fun way to find more information.

1. Go to www.factsurfer.com.

2. Enter "desert animals" into the search box and click Q.

3. Select your book cover to see a list of related content.

Index